I0811466

ADVENTURERS IN HISTORY

ERNEST SHACKLETON SURVIVES IN ANTARCTICA

by Janie Havemeyer
illustrated by Cesar Samaniego

Grasshopper Books, an imprint of Jump! Library by FlutterBee

Tools for Parents & Teachers

Grasshopper Books enhance imagination and introduce the earliest readers to fun storylines and illustrations. The easy-to-read text supports early reading experiences with repetitive sentence patterns and sight words.

Before Reading

- Discuss the cover illustration. What do readers see?
- Look at the glossary together. Discuss the words.

During Reading

- "Walk" through the book with the reader. Discuss new or unfamiliar words. Sound them out together.
- Look at the illustrations. When and where does the story take place? What is happening in the story?

After Reading

- Prompt the child to think more. Ask: Why do you think someone would want to explore new places? Would you like to? Why or why not?

Grasshopper Books are published by Jump!
3500 American Blvd W, Suite 150
Bloomington, MN 55431
www.jumplibrary.com

Copyright © 2026 Jump! International copyright reserved in all countries. No part of this book may be reproduced in any form without written permission from the publisher.

Jump! is a division of FlutterBee Education Group.

Library of Congress Cataloging-in-Publication Data

Names: Havemeyer, Janie, author
Samaniego, César, 1975– illustrator
Title: Ernest Shackleton survives in Antarctica
by Janie Havemeyer; Illustrated by Cesar Samaniego.
Description: Bloomington, MN: Jump!, Inc., [2026]
Series: Adventurers in history | Includes index.
Audience: Ages 7–10
Identifiers: LCCN 2025022950 (print)
LCCN 2025022951 (ebook)
ISBN 9798896621751 (hardcover)
ISBN 9798896621768 (paperback)
ISBN 9798896621775 (ebook)
Subjects: LCSH: Shackleton, Ernest Henry, Sir, 1874–1922—Travel—Antarctica—Juvenile literature | Explorers—Great Britain—Biography—Juvenile literature Endurance (Ship) —Juvenile literature | Imperial Trans-Antarctic Expedition (1914–1917) —Juvenile literature | Antarctica—Discovery and exploration—British—Juvenile literature
Classification: LCC G875.S5 H38 2026 (print)
LCC G875.S5 (ebook)
LC record available at https://lccn.loc.gov/2025022950
LC ebook record available at https://lccn.loc.gov/2025022951

Editor: Alyssa Sorenson
Direction and Layout: Anna Peterson and Molly Ballanger
Illustrator: Cesar Samaniego

Printed in the United States of America at Corporate Graphics in North Mankato, Minnesota.

Table of Contents

Trapped in Icy Waters

It is October 26, 1914. Ernest Shackleton sets sail on a wooden ship named *Endurance*. Shackleton and his **crew** of 27 men leave Argentina. They are sailing to Antarctica!

Shackleton is an **explorer**. He wants to cross Antarctica. No one has done this before. Antarctica is the coldest place on Earth. People have died exploring it. The waters around it are icy. In January, ice surrounds *Endurance*. It traps the ship. The crew is stuck.

Nine months go by. The men are still trapped. Ice presses against *Endurance*. In late October 1915, the ship cracks under the pressure. Water pours into the ship. It does not sink, but it is no longer safe.

Shackleton orders his crew to get off the ship. They take **lifeboats**, food, tents, and other **supplies** with them.

lifeboat

They set up camp on a large **ice floe**. Shackleton hopes they will drift closer to land. It is freezing cold. The men build a fire. They have tents to stay warm in. They know it is impossible to get to Antarctica now. Their only hope is to **survive** and find help.

Weeks go by. The men play cards and sing songs. They hunt seals for food.

On November 21, 1915, the crew watches *Endurance* sink.

In April, strong waves smash against the crew's ice floe. It starts to crack. It is not safe to stay there. Shackleton orders his men to leave on the three lifeboats.

Shackleton's boat leads the way. The sea is choppy. The wind roars. They see land in the distance. It is Elephant Island! This island is off Antarctica's northeast coast.

The crew rows hard for seven days. They reach the island. But no one is there to help them. They still have no way home.

Shackleton knows there are **whaling stations** on South Georgia Island. People are there. The island is 800 miles (1,290 kilometers) away. Shackleton and five other men set off from Elephant Island to find help.

They sail for 16 days. Temperatures drop, and ice forms on the boat. Strong winds toss their boat. Gigantic waves crash into them. Water pours over the deck. Everyone gets soaked.

They land on South Georgia Island's coast. It is rocky. Shackleton and two other men set off to find a whaling station.

The men climb steep, snowy mountains. They slide down **glaciers**. They lower themselves down a wall of ice on ropes. They finally see a whaling station. They find help at last!

Shackleton boards a ship called *Yelcho*. It sets off to rescue the rest of the crew. It reaches Elephant Island on August 30, 1916. The men cheer when they spot Shackleton. They are saved! Shackleton was a brave leader. He kept everyone alive during this dangerous adventure.

Endurance Crew's Timeline

October 26, 1914
Shackleton and his crew board *Endurance* in Argentina.

January 18, 1915
Ice traps *Endurance* in the Weddell Sea.

November 21, 1915
Endurance sinks.

April 9, 1916
The crew leaves the ice floe in three lifeboats.

April 16, 1916
The crew lands on Elephant Island.

April 24, 1916
Shackleton and five men set sail for South Georgia Island.

May 10, 1916
Shackleton and his men make it to South Georgia Island.

August 30, 1916
Yelcho rescues Shackleton's crew on Elephant Island.

Shackleton's Journey

Shackleton and his crew got stuck in ice before reaching Antarctica. How did they get back? Take a look!

To Learn More

FACT SURFER

Finding more information is as easy as 1, 2, 3.

1. Go to www.factsurfer.com
2. Enter "**Ernest Shackleton**" into the search box.
3. Choose your book to see a list of websites.

Glossary

crew: People who work on a ship.

explorer: Someone who travels in order to discover things.

glaciers: Slow-moving bodies of ice.

ice floe: A floating piece of ice.

lifeboats: Boats carried on a larger ship that are used in emergencies.

supplies: Materials needed to do something.

survive: To stay alive.

whaling stations: Places where hunted whales are cut up and stored.

Index